FROM THE BOWELS OF MY HEART

A collection of poems by
Ryan McCabe

With illustrations by Aidan Terry

ISBN 978-1-7331663-5-5

This book is dedicated to you.

Just kidding.

FROM
THE
BOWELS
OF
MY
HEART

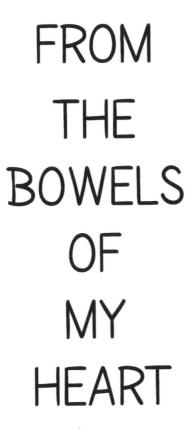

SNOW

It's snowing! It's snowing!
What a marvelous sight!
Wait, how's it indoors?
Oh, I have Dandruff. Right.

DOWN THERE

Alone in his castle
way up high in the clouds,
the little boy pondered
what life was like on the ground.

CIRCUS IN THE SKY

A bubbling bed
of foam and of cream,
where the wandering mind
may actively dream.
A home for ideas
to silently scale
along mighty mountains
that are both sharp and frail.
Wispy waves
span the floor of the sky,
to fill a vast canyon
rearranging by eye,
and buoyantly bound
like a merry-go-round.
If only my feet
weren't stuck on the ground.

WARTS

Sarah's fairytale said
that with true love's first kiss
an ordinary toad
could turn into a prince.

How she longed for romance
so, she ran to the bog
and proceeded to kiss
every toad and each frog.

When they just wouldn't change,
hopped around and ate flies,
Sarah ripped up her book
and denounced all its lies.

Though she left quite upset,
darting out of the bog,
at least next time she'll know
that a frog's just a frog.

THE GOLEM

On the hill he just sat,
his head filled with chagrin,
for this giant made of rocks
wished to play violin.

FOUND

I danced my dance,
and the crowd went away.
Everyone, except you.
You decided to stay.

MIDDLE SCHOOL ROMANCE

Shall I compare thee
to a nostril in my nose?
I shall.
I picked you.

DON'T

Don't tell me what to do!

Don't yell at me, brat!

Don't touch, I'll sue!

Don't say that!

Don't stare!

DON'T!

So, does anyone want to play frisbee?

WHO'S WHO

There's a finger-wagging frenzy
and they love to tell you "No!"
They put up borders everywhere,
then say which way to go.
Now, should you step outside the line
another frenzy's there,
but should you stand atop it
they are easy to compare.

MISSED CALL

I swear, I meant to call you back!
My phone fell on the subway track!
While I spoke with the MTA,
a rat found it and ran away
then dropped it in some greenish goo,
where suddenly it grew, and grew!
It sprouted teeth, and feet, and arms,
attacked the city causing harm.
It damaged malls, and ravaged bars,
Turned up its brightness, blinding cars.
So, see that's why I couldn't call.
It's really not my fault at all!
I pray this message makes it through.
I swear, I want to talk to you!

19

TOO MANY TOYS

He had knights for a castle
Bricks for a fort
Balls he could juggle
Ships and a port
Cannons with water
A drum he could play
Fake swords for fighting
Some tops and a tray
Trucks with big wheels
A mechanical dog
A wood cabin set,
which had multiple logs
A room filled with toys
weighing one metric ton
and the boy never played
with a single one.

MATTER

You can steal from my books,
borrow my rhymes,
crack at that vault
that no one will find.
Take my possessions,
it won't matter to me.
The only true thief in life
is my own memory.

BOX PEOPLE

Box People spend all day
in a tiny little box.
They wear the same old pair of pants
and the same old dirty socks.
They almost never go outside.
They're afraid to see the sun.
A day alone indoors
is a day that's fun.
A shame they never crack
the lid. No hide, nor hair.
To think of all that's in that box
that they could share.

LOST

The Ambassadors measure,
crunch numbers, and write
while we drink and share stories
under cover of night.
So, to seem safely eager,
it's in them we confide.
But they've clocked out already,
leaving just you and I.

OASIS

Wrapped in you
is a moment free from time.
A stone in a pond,
unmoved by the current.

Acceptance
as my first friend swaddled,
and my last
shall lay to rest.

I lie with you,
and the world goes dark.

For you are, to me,
a warm embrace
the likes,
I've never known.

VACANCY

How long does it take
to get used to the silence?
The past and the present
caught in unending violence.
A month, maybe two?
Or a year? Will that do?
How hard to pretend
the world spins without you.

EVE

My tears could fill a river
and I'd name it after you.
I'd bathe until the sun went down
and my skin began to blue.
By day, you would be gone,
my body warm upon the sand.
Without you, I could never swim.
I finally understand.

FLEETING

In the blink of an eye

we are here and then gone,

and so, it continues,

on and on.

Though there won't be another

you nor I.

I'm glad that we met,

there's no true goodbye.

You're always with me,

and I'm always there too.

A moment in time

that will never undo.

In the blink of an eye

we are here and then gone,

and so, it continues,

on and on.

AFTER

The Wicked Witch was vanquished,
but her sister missed her dearly.
She sought out the authorities
to see the matter clearly.

Though Charming was quite handsome
he had proved to be a bore.
He seldom helped around the house;
just sung of blood and gore.

And freedom came at quite a price,
the Damsel soon would learn.
The servants watched her every move
to quell her dad's concern.

Turns out the dragon, which was slain,
was actually endangered,
and so no more were ever seen,
which bummed out all the Maesters.

Ever After carried on,
though with a touch of gray,
For despite the story's end
there'd be another day.

DIVORCE

The sidewalk collapsed
at the crack of a bell,
and without light or direction
he fell deeper through hell...

THE DARK DOOR

In the darkest of corners
the penitent man cries
behind a solitary door
with a crimson red eye.
Where a veil of fog,
and endless night,
smother the shimmer
of virtue's might.
Whips, and straps,
blindfolds, and chains,
await any man
who marks himself brave.
Curiosity alone
is the entrance fee,
but once you're inside
you may never leave.

DOUBT

Doubt wears many masks,
but behind each one
is the same reflection
since your journey's begun.

WRATH

The one-eyed witch
brewed a cauldron of hate
and demanded the lives
that had made her irate.

While she cackled and cursed
the pot burst into flame,
and the witch's black soul
was the first to be claimed.

A LETTER TO MY HEART

I've given you away before,
then found you on the floor.
It makes it harder every time
to share you more and more.
But if, perchance, I squeeze too tight
I fear that you may pop,
and so, I will keep looking
for someone who wants to swap.

A KING'S JOURNAL

They crowned him a King
And still it was there
He conquered his foes
And still it was there
He wed a white rose
And still it was there
She gave him six heirs
And still it was there
The townspeople sang
And still it was there
Prosperity reigned
And still it was there
He slumped on his throne
And still it was there
A Kingdom at ease
And still it was there.

THE WHISPER CHILDREN

Oh, reader, beware of that quiet space,
where The Whisper Children silently pace.
In a ghost town, you see, with blank broadsides,
their books hold no words and their songs no rhymes.
Tread carefully, please. They're quick to offense,
and will come for your voice with no recompense.
Oh, reader, I warn you, their promise is hollow.
There's nothing the Children will not simply swallow.
So, heed my words and watch what you say,
As I write this now, they are headed my way

THE WOMAN IN BLACK

Her hair slick as oil.
Her lips black as ink.
She strolled down the carpet,
and with each step I'd sink.

A glint of emerald
stark from porcelain skin.
I loosened my tie
to release heat within.

My nostrils flared,
seared by fragrance's reach.
She nested beside me
and clung like a leech.

Then she whispered a kiss
gently into my ear,
and with one puff of smoke,
suddenly disappeared.

Though I searched the whole banquet,
she'd escaped with her tease.
The woman in black
had my heart and my keys.

PLASTIQUE

Her face plastered upon the wall
enchanting takers, one and all.
A remedy to help you hide
the discomfort you feel inside
A dash of paint
to slather on.
Just flick your wrist
and there, it's gone.
Apply your blush,
then wake and stare
back at her face,
which now you wear.

NOTHING TO FEAR

Banshees hid beneath her bed.
Creatures claimed her closet.
Demons held her dresser drawers,
fiends the bathroom faucet.
But spectres never spooked her,
rather Sally slept content.
She saw an opportunity
and charged the monsters rent.

AS I AM

To see my most ugly
and not turn away,
now that's love, I tell you.
For that I could stay.

THE BALLAD OF BARRISTON
29 | 5'11" | Eyes: Blue

There are romances born
from true love's first kiss,
a magical spell,
or a monster's quelled hiss,
but this tale contained
no fantastical trap,
rather this one began
with a dating app...

BREATHE

He waited morning, noon, and night,
for her to call or text or write.
The day shortly became a week,
his mailbox never made a creak.

She's busy, she is out with friends.
Perhaps she's on a cell phone cleanse!
He figured he'd just wait outside,
and wait he did, until he died.

And gone he was, without a word.
A life spent waiting, how absurd!
What tragedy, this senseless death.
So, heed this tale.
Don't hold your breath.

PAST YOUR NOSE

Could it be that we should wait
before we speak aloud?
For maybe what we first believe
is not always so sound.

Hey! Sorry for not responding. Crazy week. Wanna get lunch soon?

REDACTED ████████

████████ LOVE

It's ████████████

████████ undoubtedly

████ true ████████

████ that ████████

████████████ I ████

really ████████████

████ love ████████████

████████████ you.

GHOSTED

What happened to those words
I whispered gently in your ear?
Did they lose their way
or did they simply disappear?
I'm waiting for an answer,
but the silence is unclear,
and makes me question all I shared
that I hold near and dear.

REALLY RIPPED JIM

Not a word of his was heard,
so Jim did something quite absurd.
He lifted weights, then cars, then trees,
then bungalows with plenty ease.
He lifted condos, then a yacht,
and pretty soon grew quite a lot.
Now, Jim is no longer a mouse,
but it's a problem for his spouse.
'Cause while Jim's
louder than before,
he cannot fit
inside the door.

ONION BOY

Though he'd greet passers-by
with a "Hello" or "Hi!"
Onion Boy couldn't help
but make everyone cry.

One puff of perfume,
something fragrant and cheap,
but now, Onion Boy's scent
made even him weep.

THEAGONY

Medusa took one selfie,
and was quickly turned to stone.
So, no Helena. You're too young
to have a mobile phone.

LEMONS

The toothless zombie did his best,
but couldn't bite into man's breast.
His faith, however, never swayed.
He'd make these lemons lemonade.
Now, zombies walk throughout the land
to have a sip from his smoothie stand
In fact, they're hiring! Ain't that grand?
Come on, please won't you lend a hand?

DATING

Another arrow fired
and another arrow failed.
I gave companionship a try,
but loneliness prevailed.
Surprisingly, I'm not upset,
tomorrow I'll aim higher.
Who knows, perhaps I'll even be
in someone's line of fire!

THE BUTLER DID IT

The burglars broke in with their bags for the haul,
while just 'round the corner he prepped for the brawl.
With a broom by his side he charged like a boar!
They thought it a bluff and were swept to the floor.
Yes, he bested the bandits. Bound the brigade!
Then fetched a dust pan for the mess that they'd made.
He booted and brushed each brute out the door,
and assured them next time they'd be doing his chores.
So, beware fellow robbers, safe crackers, and crooks.
If there's somewhere you're bound, go and get second looks.
Check for booby traps, trip-wires, landmines, and hounds,
but most of all, make sure no Butler's around!

MR. BLUE

"The world's out to get me,"
thinks Mr. Blue,
and I'll tell you this,
it's true!
That's why I'm writing this to you,
'cause if you see that Mr. Blue,
be sure
you get him too!

PUZZLE MAN

Though Puzzle Man looked both high and low,
his missing pieces would not show.
He looked beneath his queen-sized bed,
and nearly lost a piece of head.
He searched between the couch and found,
some fingertips were missing now.
"When will my problems ever end?
If only I was like my friends."
It frustrates Puzzle Man, you see,
to be the one who's incomplete.

RORY

All the penguins told Rory
that he'd never fly,
so he saved every penny
and now travels sky-high.

CAPTAIN COULDN'T

Captain Couldn't always tried,
but never saved the day.

He'd stand up to the villains,
and be swiftly put away.

In spite of all his failure though,
he held his head up high.

For while success escaped him,
he was never scared to try.

SILVER TOOTH SUE

The glint of silver from a toothy grin
let the townspeople know Sue was at it again.
She did business each day with an iron six-shooter
to each teller's dismay like an old-fashioned looter.
Throughout the frontier, saloons feared of a drought,
for Sue loved her root beer and would clean the house out.
Disgruntled outlaws, and eager guns,
always sought after Sue, but were quickly undone.
For the price on her head was growing quite often,
those stupid to try though soon needed a coffin.
Then one day the Marshall caught a wabblin' jaw,
who told of Sue's hideout and prompted the law.
Six rifles, four pistols, and a Marshall lay wait,
for the moment when Sue would approach her front gate.
And what happened next I can't rightfully say,
but for sure, no one lives who was there on that day.
Rumors spread far and wide, notably in El Paso,
from inside an old bar which was called Broken Lasso,
where a card sharp, they say, who was hustling at Gin
cleaned a few people out with a silvery grin.

THE OLD MAN IN ME

The old man in me wants to earn a degree,
then he'll look for a house with a swing on a tree
that he'll buy with his job, and serve corn on the cob
to the whole family with an entrée of squab.
This old man cannot wait to try beer and to date,
and to stay up past bedtime at quarter to eight.
All the fun it will be eating sweets merrily,
with nobody to tell you "Eat more broccoli!"
He's quite eager to drive and yet still only five,
though he's lost in the joy that old age will derive.
So, he'll lay down today for he cannot delay
the excitement of waking to be old and gray.
Yes, the old man in me. That is just what I'll be!
Oh, to think of the doors that will open for me...

OFFICE PLANT

Whose grip can you shake
and what friends will you make
when your hands are glued to a desk? Oh, my!
When your hands are glued to a desk!

In what space are you free
to get vitamin D
when your butt is stuck in a chair? Uh-oh!
When your butt is stuck in a chair.

Where can you go,
and how will you grow
when your feet are stuck to the floor? Please no!
When your feet are stuck to the floor!

THE WOLF

The Wolf gnawed on some grass
without uttering a peep,
and wondered if those nearby
turned him into a sheep.

THE FASTEST

How hard we all strive
to be the fastest alive.
And yet, it's clear we can't see
what a lonely life that would be.

THE MOLE

They're digging their tunnels.
They're hatching a scheme.
They've damaged my soil,
and assembled a team.
I tell you, those moles,
They're planning a raid,
and intend to run off with
the produce I've made!
What's that? You wonder
how all this is known?
Well, let me just say
I've a mole of my own.

ACCEPTANCE

The things we bury deep inside,
shield from the sun and choose to hide,
have ways of slipping through the cracks,
while leaving small unwanted tracks.
So, tell yourself that they're not there,
and watch them grow to your despair.
Or face them, and in their embrace,
accept what you cannot erase.

BOY IN A BOTTLE

Despite all the fun,
despite all the games,
he couldn't escape
from the cloud in his brain.

EXPECTATIONS

Oh brain, why do I entertain
the thoughts that simply bring me pain?
I focus hard on what is not
instead of all that I have got.
I let desire scratch and tear
my self-esteem till it's not there.
I think we need to have a talk,
about this mental laughingstock.
We've gone in circles, you and I,
but there's something I'd like to try.
Why don't we practice gratitude
instead of a bad attitude?
Why don't we make some room to fail?
Perfection's an elusive whale.
The curse of not enough
is all it takes to wreck what's pleasant,
So rather let's just take a second
to enjoy the present.

THE AWESOME POSSUM

The Awesome Possum woke up,
and he launched right out of bed!
He took off for an awesome day
with awesome things ahead!
He skated at an awesome park
among his awesome friends!
He nailed an awesome trick
with complicated twists and bends!
He settled for an awesome nap,
then had an awesome snack!
He shredded his guitar
and sang without a single crack!
He took an awesome hike,
and then he leapt out of a jet!
He flew past a volcano,
where he broke an awesome sweat!
He went back to his awesome house,
got into awesome bed,
then saw a shooting star,
an awesome thought inside his head.
The possum prayed upon that star
before he went to sleep.
He wished for just one normal day,
and did so awesomely.

MULTIPLE ME'S

Ah! The ease of many me's,
my worries handled in a breeze.
No birthdays missed, no book unread.
Timely answers to each thread.
I'd multi-task, I'd go explore.
I'd learn to paint, and dance, and more!
To think of all that I'd get done
with many me's instead of one.
There's just one problem I foresee:
there's no telling which me I'd be.

ONE LAST BITE

Maybe just one more yellow.
Maybe just one more blue.
Maybe just one more handful
to see the day through.
Ah, the sweet taste of rainbows.
Each color's great too!
How could anything so good
ever be bad for you?

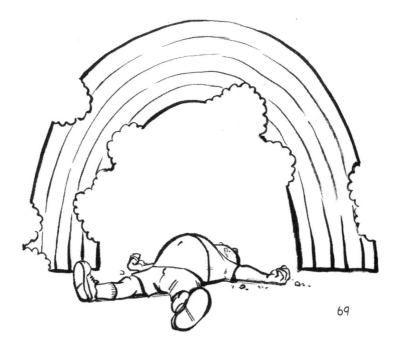

THE DANCE

The ballerina on my screen
is summoned with a click.
She pirouettes, she then plies.
She lifts a slender kick.
I gape at her with bated breath,
she frisks across the stage.
Oh, how I wish to dance again,
an itch I must assuage.

THE GIRL OF MY DREAMS

That moon-kissed beauty,
the girl of my dreams,
she always knows what to say.

She could take any rain cloud
over my head
and easily shoo it away.

Her eyes meet mine
and every time
my heart prepares to erupt.

I take her hand
and ask her name,
but that's when I wake up.

FRIEND WANTED

I'd like to take an ad out for I'd like to find a friend,
a person whose reliable and free on the weekends.
I have a list of qualities that hopefully you match.
So, if this sounds like you,
then please reply to my dispatch!
I'm looking for a person who's no bigger than 6' 2".
A friendly, charismatic sort, who can be mellow too!
A witty joker, who is also serious at times.
A homebody who also likes to go on outdoor climbs.
This person must have matching socks,
should answer every message,
although I'd like some space as well,
so no one too obsessive.
They have to like the films I do,
to that there's no exception.
They also must be honest for I will not do deception.
I need you to believe in ghosts,
and help me with my studies.
I'm sure that if you can comply
we'll be the best of buddies!
That should be everything I want,
Oh, wait! They must eat cheese.
I don't think that's asking too much,
reply at your own ease!

TIMELY

Early bird Fred,
who was always ahead,
hopped into a coffin
and claimed to be dead.
Mourners gave him a prod,
shook their heads, "What a fraud!"
Although Fred felt divine
for he soon met his God.

DEER TEACH,

To the teacher who said I can't write good,
I told you I am misunderstood.
You thaught I wouldn't amount to much,
and yet my book here's got a bunch.
It seems I'm quite the writer to.
I'll bet that just plum bothers you.
Two think I've got one book now done.
And how many have you written? None!
So their you have it!
Read them and wheat.
I'll toast you're glorious defeat.
Its not easy for me to say
but you're work made me
what I'm today.
So thanks for doubting me back than.
Now, look how well I write with pen!
Im sure youll be a writer to.
Just lower your standars. That'll due.

TO WHOM

Do I do this for me?
Or for you? I've no clue.
If not me, and not you,
well then please tell me who.
I'm sure you think one thing
while someone thinks another.
Perhaps we should sit
and share notes with each other.
'Cause frankly I'm lost,
won't you please tell me true,
who is it you address
when you do what you do?

BEATBOX BOT

Beatbox Bot just loves to rap,
and he'd like to say hello.
So, pump up the volume, grab a seat
Kick back, and enjoy the show...

"Boop –
Bop –
BEEP Boop,
111 ~ 0!"

Wait a minute bot!
Please, hold that thought.
There are kids here,
don't you know?

"Boop –
Boop –
BEEP Boop
111 ~ 0!"

Folks please don't go!
There's still more show.
Bot, why'd you have to
say that bro?

WRITER'S BLOCK

The ideas were ready
to charge the blockade
and escape through the walls
of their thick-headed cave.
When suddenly, they ...
Um.
When suddenly ...
They ...

INSPIRATION

Stop honking at me!
Turn left! Go around!
I'm working on something
that's deeply profound.
What's your hurry, pal?
Just wait one more sec'.
The iron is hot
and I need to strike quick!

ACE PENCIL TECHNICIAN

The crowd took their seats and each driver their place,
for what soon was to be an incredible race.
There were thunderbirds, raptors, spitfires, and vipers.
Roadsters and beetles with large windshield wipers.
Hatchbacks, convertibles, go-karts, and tanks.
Automobiles outfitted with cranks.
Muscle cars, carriages, tractors, and vans.
Horse-drawn buggies! Catamarans!
And all that I had was a bike at my side.
A custom design I had crafted with pride.
My rivals were fierce, this was no exaggeration,
but none of them quite had my knack for illustration.

FLEA THE TREE

This is a tree.
Its name is Flea.
And Flea is quite upset with me.
I wrote a book for all to see,
and now Flea is an amputee.
Hyperbole?
Well, not to Flea.
It's part of Flea that you now read.
Unless you read digitally,
in which case, Flea is quite happy.
But if you're feeling bad for Flea,
and wish to make amends like me,
the solution is quite easy.
Just go outside
and plant a tree!

THE STACKS

In a forest of trees without any green,
along dotted lines he dwelt unseen.
His eyes were zeroes. His fingers were ones.
And tomorrow's demands were today's to be done.
His world was paper. Paper planes, paper skies.
Tall paper towers where paper cranes fly.
He stacked it all day and when nine turned to five,
he would sit and just wait for more reams to arrive.
Then he'd get back to stacking, so towers could grow,
and this task was his life....
To what end, I don't know.

THE OBSERVER

There's an Eye in the sky
keeping watch if you lie,
and then what happens next...
Well, it's best to comply.
Be sure not to offend.
Oh, my Eye! Play pretend.
Act like everyone else
then you too can ascend.

LITTLE MICHAEL

Little Michael wore blue,
but his parents wore red.
Why he wouldn't wear red,
made no sense in their heads.

So, they sent him away
to a camp where he'd stay,
and then learn to wear red,
though he liked blue instead.

Michael's folks grew upset,
so to stave off their fret
they drove out to the camp
just to check on their scamp.

Camp assured them "No blue."
He's inside learning too!
Now tell me, doesn't Michael
look happy to you?

HEAT

Oh, angry boy
what will you do
to quell that rage
inside of you?

Breathe in and out?
Go for a walk?
Or maybe find a friend
and talk?

This world still has
a place for you.
The journey's rough,
but you'll get through.

Oh, angry boy
please don't dismay.
Tomorrow is another day.

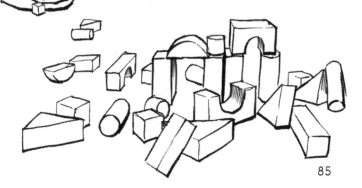

INDEPENDENCE

I DON'T CARE WHAT YOU THINK!
I AM ME, AND I'M PROUD.
I WILL STAND UP AND SHOUT,
AND I DON'T CARE HOW LOUD.
NO, I DON'T NEED APPROVAL
ONE BIT, IN THE LEAST.
Now, do me a favor,
rate this book online, please?

MIRROR MIRROR

The Magic Mirror in the stall
wished it was anywhere else at all.

JOE

I knew a bear who worked a job
and loved his morning brew.
He'd punch in early every day
to prep his coffee queue.
He sat and periodically
reached for another sip,
the strong effect this beverage had,
it almost made him skip!
One morning he arrived quite late
and much to his surprise,
the machine in the kitchen
he did find immobilized.
Now, what the bear did then,
well goodness me, was awfully rude.
I heard that he was quite upset,
and threw a feral 'tude.

NIGH

Help! What horror!
We're trapped inside.
The sun's at high noon
and there's nowhere to hide!
For the love of God,
please rescue me!
I won't last much longer
without an AC.

THE CARDBOARD CADET

In his parents' garage
a costume took shape
with the use of some scissors,
some boxes, and tape...
The Cardboard Cadet
then burst onto the scene!
A corrugated hero
to challenge those mean!
He darted outdoors,
for he'd finished his training,
but no one had mentioned
that outside it was raining.

NIGHT OUT

I'll leave the house, but first thing's first,
I need a canteen for my thirst!
However, I could spill a bit.
I'll take a rag to handle it!
Though what a slog, to bring a rag.
I guess, I'll throw it in my bag.
Although, I could get hungry too.
I'll pack a snack and then I'm through.
Wait, what's the time?
Oh, so it's dark.
I'll need a flashlight to embark.
No batteries. That's all she wrote...
Unless I can find the remote.
Perhaps it's on the couch. Let's see.
Well, I must say. This is comfy.
I think I'll sit down for a while.
Arriving late is now in style.
Just one more thing, and then I'm there,
I need to find something to wear.

TSUNDOKU

There is a stack of books,
which you can see beneath my bed,
it measures one mile high
with novels I have never read.
Some comics from the local store,
romance novellas too,
a few things from the library,
dusty and overdue.
My parents signal "Dinner time,"
with hopes I'll leave the sky,
and tempting as that is
I still have many books to buy!

MR. INCONSIDERATE

He's thoughtless in his actions.
He's heedless in his deals.
He often eats the food he finds
from other people's meals.
He drives the world insane,
a man I'd frankly like to smother.
Yes, Mr. Inconsiderate
acknowledges no other.
I wonder how he got that way.
Why is he such a pill?
Did something happen in his past
that sent his faith downhill?
He does only what pleases him;
he'd cheat his own dear mother.
Now, tell me how you stand someone
who's ignorant to others?

MULISH

The whipping winds still whistle
through the cracks in canyons high,
and sing a song of stubbornness
beneath the desert sky.

A song about a cactus
with its roots inside the ground
so deeply that it never moved
from daybreak to sundown.

A pointed plant obdurate
in its cause to never change,
and so, it grew thick thistles
to keep company at range.

And lonely was the stubborn plant
for loneliness it sought,
but while its neighbors touched the sky
this one was doomed to squat.

THE OTHER SIDE

Through the misty film glass
of the door by your side
you hear snickers and whispers
that all seem to chide.

Though you try to avoid them
shapes flicker and howl,
while on each sound you linger
dreaming up things quite foul.

Are they speaking of me?
Do they think that I smell?
Am I doing my best?
Will they bid me farewell?

I don't mean to sound selfish,
but it's hard to ignore
when you are the one
just outside of the door.

ANXIETY

WhirLinG wInDing WhiSking bRain
wrIthing wHomPing WelComed StraIn
A whiPpeD-uP wHuppIng wipEout
whiLe mY foCus wRestles wriGglIng
aT the waSteful wHistled whIning
waLlowing in wRath and wOe.

MORTALITY

Daniel the skull kid
just wanted to play,
but he scared off the others
'cause he reeked of decay.

HAUNTED

I ended the fight
with my teeth tightly grit,
while a candle alight
faded until it quit.
Maybe death's not the end,
but don't ask, I can't say.
Instead speak to the voices
that won't go away.

EL DORADO

You found El Dorado!
Why the long face?
Wasn't this what you wanted
in the first place?

TO FLY

You can batten down hatches,
secure all of your doors,
shut away danger
you're trying to ignore.
Board up each window,
seek refuge from pain,
but how else will you fly
inside a hurricane?

RAIN

Oh, how I simply hate the rain.
It's presence causes me such pain.
My shoes get wet,
my toes quite cold,
I barely make it down the road.
My books get soaked,
my glasses fog,
I suddenly smell like a dog.
If only there was no more rain
I'd never be upset again.
Aha! That's it. It's settled, done.
I'll go somewhere with only sun!
Next stop, more sun. One ticket, please!
At last, my life may be at ease.

SUN

Goodness, how I loathe the sun.
To think, I dreamed this would be fun.
I'm always thirsty,
out of breath,
my clothes are wet from my own sweat.
Outdoors, I must put lotion on.
Indoors, all able fans are on.
If only this place had some rain,
I'd never be upset again.
Perhaps, I never should have moved,
and caught this crummy attitude.
One ticket! Yes, for the next train.
At last, life will be right as rain.

HARMONY

The Fire, Water, Earth, and Sky,
all had a simple wager
to see which of the four of them
could cultivate more favor.
So Fire cooked delicious food,
while Water gave them fish.
The Earth made wood for shelter
and the Sky a place to wish.
The elements soon found
that each was praised like any other,
and grew dissatisfied
so, they all turned on one another.
Fire burned Earth's shelters down,
Water drowned the flames.
Trees blocked out the Sky,
while winds uprooted all Earth's claims.

Chaos then unfolded
and the people lived in fear.
A shadow grasped the world
as nature's balance disappeared.
The elements, ashamed to see
the harvest of their greed,
abandoned their own interests
and aligned for one last deed.
Fire chased the shadows off.
Water cleansed the ground.
Earth then sprouted crops, which
Sky had scattered all around.
Balance was restored;
at last the elements each saw
that each needed the other
to maintain the natural law.

OUTSIDE

They told me all that I would see
was famine, war, and poverty.
Those things were there,
make no mistake,
but no one mentioned beauty.

MAJOR

Major the pug was a vigilant guard
and he seldom batted an eye.
A shame that in spite of his dutiful watch
he let so many things pass by.

DAVID

To walk among giants
may make you feel small,
but I'll bet you can do things
they can't reach at all.

ONE-SIDED

With every letter that I write
my feet approach the floor.
With every call or invite
they dip down a little more.

With every deed, or helping hand,
suggestion, joke, or chore.
I watch my feet sink closer
towards a truth I can't ignore.

It's every unread letter,
and each day with no reply,
that makes me wonder where you went,
and why I even try.

LIFE

LIfe. Life. LIfe. Life. LIfe. Life. LIfe. Life. LIfe.
Life. LIfe. Life. LIfe. Life. LIfe. Life. LIfe. Life.
LIfe. Life. LIfe. Life. LIfe. Life. LIfe. Life. LIfe.
Life. LIfe. Life. LIfe. Life. LIfe. Life. LIfe. Life.
LIfe. Life. LIfe. Life. LIfe. Life. LIfe. Life. LIfe.
Life. LIfe. Life. LIfe. Life. LIfe. Life. LIfe. Life.
LIfe. Life. LIfe. Life. LIfe. Life. LIfe. Life. LIfe.
Life. LIfe. Life. LIfe. Life. LIfe. Life. LIfe. Life.
LIfe. Life. LIfe. Life. LIfe. Life. LIfe. Life. LIfe.
Life. LIfe. Life. LIfe. Life. LIfe. Life. LIfe. Life.
LIfe. Life. LIfe. Life. LIfe. Life. LIfe. Life. LIfe.
Life. LIfe. Life. LIfe. Life. LIfe. Life. LIfe. Life.
Life. LIfe. Life. LIfe. Life. LIfe. Life. LIfe. Life.
LIfe. Life. LIfe. Life. LIfe. Life. LIfe. Life. LIfe.
Life. LIfe. Life. LIfe. Life. LIfe. Life. LIfe. Life.
LIfe. Life. LIfe. Life. LIfe. Life. LIfe. Life. LIfe.
Life. LIfe. Life. LIfe. Life. LIfe. Life. LIfe. Life.
Life. LIfe. Life. LIfe. Life. LIfe. Life. LIfe.
Life. Life. LIfe. Life. Lif

WHERE THE SKY MEETS THE SEA

Castles, and kings,
horses, and knights,
fade like the sands
swept away by the tide.
And so, too, shall I go
where the sky meets the sea,
and one day you will join,
and there we both shall be.
If your still on the shore,
do not rush, grab some sand,
and build, while you can,
in your small plot of land.
Build castles for Kings,
Queens, and the like.
Horses to carry some
battle-worn knights.
Build until finally
you sit down to see,
that strange little line
where the sky meets the sea.

THOSE WHO PAVED THE WAY

Will you join me in a moment
for the ones who paved the way,
and thank them for the work they did
we pass by every day?
Some names do not make placards.
and some stars will go unseen.
Some sidewalks seem to never end,
all paved behind the scenes.
And just as sure as you or I
will breathe a gulp of air,
we sometimes take for granted
things our eyes forget are there.
Now take a moment, any length,
to sit back and review
the people you are grateful for
who paved the way for you.

NOTE TO THE EDITOR

I have an issue plain to see

for while I choose words carefully

sometimes they're written speedily

and maintenance is called.

A specialist then takes a peek,

someone to fix my mental leak,

since often things just need a tweak.

Thank God for editors.

AN INVITATION

I've made a space that's just for you
to do whatever you'd like to.
Grab a pencil, brush, or pen,
let your mind unwind and then
feast your eyes on what you've done!
Perhaps you'll share or tell no one.
Whatever you decide to do,
just promise me you'll follow through.
The hardest thing to do is start,
whenever you're creating art.
And so, I leave it up to you.
Next page is yours. Good luck, adieu.

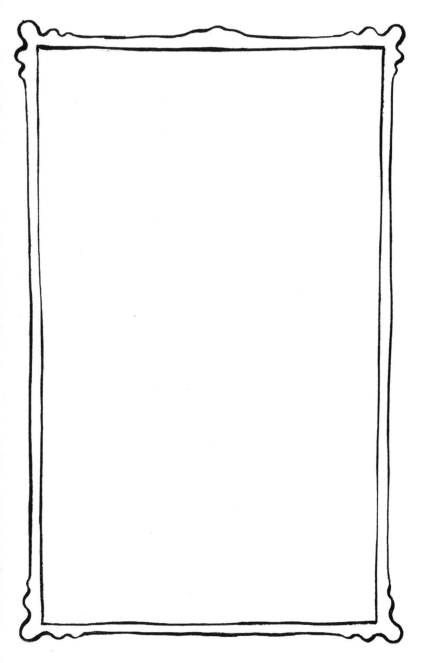

Acknowledgments

To my family, and all of the other people in my corner.
Thank you for your warmth, laughter, support,
guidance, patience, and most of all, thank you for
the memories.

To Aidan, without whom, none of this would have been
possible.

ABOUT THE AUTHOR

Ryan McCabe is an award-winning filmmaker and writer from Toledo, Ohio. A graduate of NYU's Tisch School of the Arts, he has since written content for Whoopi Goldberg, as well as contributed to projects for NETFLIX, children's entertainment, and feature film adaptations for theatrical release.

Ryan currently resides in Los Angeles where he works at DreamWorks Animation.

FROM THE BOWELS OF MY HEART is his debut book.

ABOUT THE ILLUSTRATOR

Aidan Terry is an animator and illustrator based in Los Angeles, CA. An alumnus of NYU's Tisch School of the Arts, he is currently working on the Netflix animated feature "Over the Moon," directed by Disney Legend Glen Keane, as well as animating on Disney Legend Andreas Deja's independent short film, "Mushka."

Both projects are due to be released in late 2020.

$12.95

ISBN 978-1-7331663-5-5

51295>

Made in the USA
San Bernardino, CA
23 February 2020

64655185R00069